# PUMPKINS AND PARTY THEMES

## 50 DIY DESIGNS
### TO BRING YOUR HALLOWEEN EXTRAVAGANZA TO LIFE

ROXANNE RHOADS

Skyhorse Publishing

*The themes, decor, party activities, and costume ideas in this book were created with adults in mind. The use of sharp or otherwise potentially harmful tools and materials should only be done by adults or under adult supervision.*

To my mother, ClaraBelle, thank you for sharing your crafty genes with me. Because of you I love to create beautiful things.

To my wonderful family—Robert, Tim, Ari, and Robby—thank you for all the fun family pumpkin carving nights that inspired so many of my pumpkin design ideas.

# CONTENTS

# INTRODUCTION

Welcome to *Pumpkins and Party Themes*.

In this book, you'll find ten unique Halloween party themes that are showcased with tips, tricks, and ideas for coordinating decor, party activities, and costumes, plus five DIY pumpkin designs for each party theme. That's fifty pumpkin DIYs using painting, carved designs, and mixed media craftiness.

The projects range from super simple to mid-range skill, so even if you don't consider yourself to be crafty you should be able to complete most, if not all, of the projects in this book.

I created a variety of pumpkin designs that include paint, glitter, glue, and other craftiness as well as several carved pumpkins. Not everyone likes to carve so I wanted to provide ideas and methods that everyone can enjoy. If you like to carve, some of the designs I used for painting pumpkins can easily be modified and used as carving stencils.

Feel free to mix and match designs and themes. There are many projects that can be used for multiple themes. Gothic Elegance and Blood Bash have projects that could be used for both themes. Blood Bash's Blood Splatter pumpkin would fit in great with the Zombie theme. The Zombie theme's Bloody Handprint, Brains, and Hand Reaching Out can be incorporated into the Blood Bash party if you are going for a gory style or the Brains and Hand Reaching Out can easily be background pumpkins for the Dr. Frankenstein's Laboratory theme. Edgar Allan Poe projects could be featured in Gothic Elegance and Let's Get Literary. Mina and Dracula, and the Frankie and Bride of Frankenstein silhouettes are a perfect fit for Let's Get Literary as well.

Have fun customizing a party to make it your own.

*Roxanne Rhoads*

# CHAPTER 1
# GET READY FOR HALLOWEEN

## PUMPKINS: A QUICK HISTORY

Pumpkins and Halloween go hand in hand. No other symbol is as synonymous with Halloween as a grinning *jack-o'-lantern*.

It is believed that pumpkins originated in Central America over 7,500 years ago. These original pumpkins did not resemble the bright orange variety we commonly see today. The original pumpkins were small, hard, and had a bitter taste. The pumpkins we use today are thought to have originated in North America. Seeds have been found in Mexico that are over five thousand years old.

The name pumpkin originated from the Greek word for large melon which is *pepon*. The French turned *pepon* into *pompon*. The English changed it to *pumpion*. Shakespeare referred to the *pumpion* in *The Merry Wives of Windsor*. In 1584 when the French explorer Jacques Cartier explored the St. Lawrence region of North America, he reported finding *gros melons* which translated into English as *pompions*. American colonists later changed the name to *pumpkin*.

Native Americans called pumpkins *isqoutm squash*. The squash was a staple of Native diets long before the pilgrims landed. Native people would roast long strips of pumpkin on the open fire to eat. They also dried long strips to be woven into mats.

When white settlers arrived, they learned about pumpkins and incorporated them into a variety of recipes from desserts to stews. The first pumpkin pie was created when colonists cut off the pumpkin top, removed the seeds, filled the pumpkin with honey, milk, and spices, and baked it in the hot ashes of a fire.

One of the first published American pumpkin recipes was recorded in the early 1670s in John Josselyn's *New-England's Rarities Discovered*.

## THE LEGEND OF JACK-O'-LANTERN

The legend of the jack-o'-lantern is thought to have originated in Ireland with the tale of a miserly blacksmith named Stingy Jack. Many versions of the story exist. The following is a compilation of some of these stories.

Stingy Jack was a con man. To simply call him a bad man would be an understatement. But Jack was clever and had a knack for getting out of trouble. Legend has

it Jack sold his soul to the devil for his ability to avoid the responsibility and repercussions of his actions.

One Halloween night the devil came calling. Time was up and the devil wanted what was due to him: Jack's soul.

The devil met up with Jack at a pub. Legend tells that ol' Jack had drunk way too much and his soul was on the verge of slipping away, but before the devil could collect, Jack managed to convince the devil they should have a drink together.

The devil had no money and Jack was as sly as he was stingy. He convinced the devil to turn into a sixpence so he could get that last drink. The devil's pride was his downfall; he couldn't resist showing off his shapeshifting skills so he promptly became a sixpence on the counter.

Clever Jack didn't buy a drink; he shoved that sixpence into his wallet which had a silver clasp in the shape of a cross.

He trapped the devil and wouldn't let him out until he promised not to collect Jack's soul for another ten years (some legends say it was just a year Jack bargained for).

Ten years later on Halloween night, the devil tried to collect Jack's soul again. Wandering down a lonely country road the devil suddenly appeared to Jack. They walked together and talked for a while before happening upon a tree covered in shiny red apples.

This time Jack convinced the devil to fetch him an apple. The devil stood on Jack's shoulders to climb into the tree to get the shiniest red apple they could see. While the devil was in the tree, Jack pulled out his penknife and carved a cross on the trunk of the tree trapping the devil once again.

The devil was desperate to be free. Jack's condition for getting the devil down? He made the devil promise not to come calling for his soul ever again.

When Jack died years later, he was turned away from Heaven for his sinful ways. When he tried to enter Hell, the devil said: "I cannot break my word." He had promised not to collect Jack's soul. "Go away; go back where you came from," the devil shouted at him.

"It's dark, how will I find my way?" Jack asked while munching on a turnip.

The devil threw him glowing coal which Jack placed in the turnip he had been eating. He became Jack of the Lantern, doomed to wander the earth alone for all eternity.

## JACK-O'-LANTERN HISTORY

Throughout England and Ireland, tales of ghostly lights appearing over bogs and marshes are quite common. These lights have been known as lantern men, hob-o'-lanterns, will-o'- the-wisps, corpse candles, and jack-o'-lanterns. Stories about *Jack of the Lantern* were common in the British Isles.

These pale eerie lights would bob along in the darkness like a lantern being held by someone walking. Horses tended to shy away from such lights. After a while, people learned to beware of these odd lights. Following the lights could lead a person to doom. People would get lost and sometimes sucked into a watery grave in the bogs and swamps.

Legend says if you ever encounter ol' Jack on the road you should put out your lantern so he doesn't smash it to pieces. Don't let him follow you home. Once you arrive at your destination don't take any chances, carve your own lantern and light it to stay safe from Jack.

In the English village of Hinton St George, punkies are carried through town on Halloween night. These "punkies" are special lanterns carved from large beets known as *mangel-wurzels*. Prizes are awarded for the best-carved punkie.

Old fashioned jack-o'-lanterns are truly terrifying, especially when they start to shrivel and look like shrunken heads.

In Scotland, lanterns were originally carved from turnips and in Ireland, they used turnips and potatoes. But what Americans tend to call turnips are different than traditional turnips from Europe, which are a large member of the beet family. In some areas of Scotland these were called *neeps*. The Swedish called them *rottabaggars*. In the US we call them rutabagas. So, if you want to carve a traditional lantern, grab rutabaga.

When Irish and Scottish immigrants came to the United States, they brought their Halloween (Samhain) customs with them. They quickly discovered the American pumpkin and decided it was a much better canvas for their lantern art. Large, round pumpkins with their bright colors and soft insides were perfect for carving.

In 1819, Washington Irving featured a mysterious jack-o'-lantern in *The Legend of Sleepy Hollow*. This may have further popularized the carved pumpkin and its connection to Halloween.

## PUMPKIN CARVING BASICS

Planning to carve a pumpkin?

First, you'll want to pick out your perfect pumpkin and plan your design. Choose a firm pumpkin that is free of nicks, gouges, and soft spots.

Make sure your pumpkin has a nice stem. Three to five inches is best. If your pumpkin has no stem it can rot faster.

Always carry your pumpkin from the bottom, not by the stem. The stem can break and your pumpkin can hit the ground and smash into bits.

To make sure your pumpkin stays fresh for your party, carve it no more than a day or two before the event.

Before carving, let the pumpkin sit in your house overnight so it is room temperature when you are ready to carve it. I can't tell you how many times my family has forgotten to do this and ended up trying to scoop out frozen pumpkin guts, which is no fun at all. You end up with very cold hands.

Wash the outside of the pumpkin with cool water; scrub away any clumps of dirt with a scrub brush.

Cover your work table with something to protect the surface from all the gunk and seeds. I usually put a cheap dollar store tablecloth down so we can scoop it up, guts and all, and take it outside when we're done carving. If you want to save the seeds place a large bowl on the table to put them in. I always save seeds, both for future planting and for roasted pumpkin seeds.

Gather your tools—pumpkin carving knives and saws, heavy-duty spoons or pumpkin scoopers, toothpicks, an icepick, and any other tools you may want. These can vary depending on your skill level and what

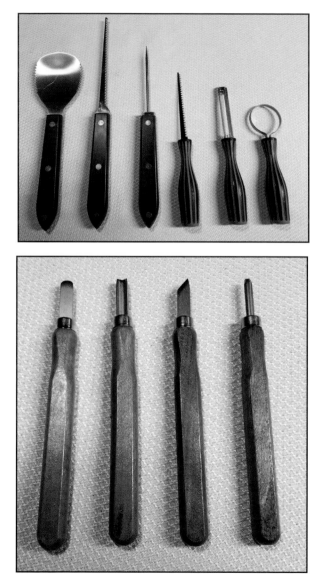

kind of design you plan to create. A knife or pumpkin saw with a serrated edge is best for carving out pieces.

The guys in my family love to break out the power tools; they use cordless drills and various bits to make holes or a Dremel to carve unique designs in the flesh. There are circular bits that will put perfect circles in your pumpkin. Sometimes an apple corer can be used for circles, depending on how firm and thick your pumpkin is.

Clay, wood, or linoleum carving tools can be used for etched designs. Some pumpkin carving kits include tools for scraping and etching designs on the outside of the pumpkin.

For the basic old-fashioned style of jack-o'-lantern carving, you'll want to start by drawing a circle either on the top or bottom of your pumpkin. If you cut the bottom open, it can be easier to place a candle or light inside. You just put the pumpkin down over the top of it. I still prefer to cut the top because I like to use the stem to help pull it open.

Always cut your opening at an angle. It makes it easier to pull the piece away from the pumpkin and seal when you put it back together. You don't want your lid to fall into your pumpkin.

Once you have created your opening, dig into the pumpkin with a scraper or spoon and start scooping out the insides of the pumpkin. You can use a thick spoon or scooper that comes with your pumpkin carving kit. There are specialty scoopers available to get the pumpkin really clean. There are even attachments for power tools.

Scrape the walls of the pumpkin until they are about an inch thick. If they are too thick, it will make carving harder. Don't leave a bunch of stringy stuff inside the pumpkin because it will rot faster.

Now you're ready to carve your design. You can either draw your design directly on the pumpkin, freestyle, or attach a stencil to the pumpkin.

Over the years I've tried many methods of transferring the stencil to the pumpkin, including the dot-to-dot poke method, carbon paper transfer, marker, tissue paper, and even leaving the stencil attached and cutting through it.

For the dot-to-dot poke method, you use a thin ice pick, sharp nail, push pin, or skewer to poke holes through the paper into your pumpkin to create a connect-the-dots design you'll follow with the blade. This method works well for real pumpkins and makes cutting so much easier. Many of the more expensive pumpkin carving tool kits contain a tool that is perfect for this.

Another nifty tool that can be used with similar results is a template wheel. Some pumpkin tool kits include these. You run the wheel over the pattern while it is attached to your pumpkin and it creates a pinprick line so you know where to cut.

If you are transferring a stencil or design to a fake pumpkin, test the pumpkin's skin by taking a piece of paper and ballpoint pen and drawing a simple design on the paper on the bottom or side of the pumpkin you are not using for your main design. Pull the paper away. Can you see the design clearly imprinted in the skin? If you can, all you need is your stencil, tape, and a ballpoint pen to trace your design onto your pumpkin.

If you can't see the design then you'll need carbon paper. Put a sheet of carbon paper transfer side down

behind your stencil and tape it all to your pumpkin. Use a ballpoint pen and press firmly while tracing the design. This will create a carbon imprint of your design on the pumpkin.

When you are ready to start cutting, start with the inner designs first.

Carve from the inside of the design outward. Saw in a steady and continuous motion. If you accidentally break a piece of the pumpkin off you can use a toothpick to reattach the piece.

Once your design is complete, you'll want to clean your pumpkin so it'll last longer. You can do this by wiping it down with a damp cloth. If you wish to preserve it you can dunk the entire pumpkin in a bucket of water mixed with ⅔ cup of bleach, or add a little bit of bleach to a spray bottle (a ratio of 4 tablespoons bleach per 16 ounces of water) and liberally apply it inside and outside of the pumpkin. This keeps mold and mildew from forming, which means it keeps rot and decay away.

If you give discarded jack-o'-lanterns to wildlife after Halloween, skip the bleach and try mixing a few drops of tea tree oil into a spray bottle of water. Squirt

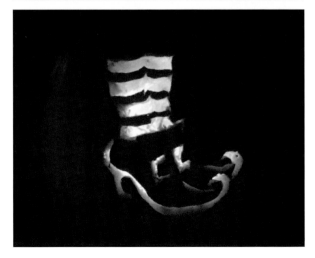

the pumpkin with this solution to help keep it fresh. You can also rub olive oil or vegetable oil on the cut areas to keep them from drying out.

Use battery-operated candles and lights instead of real candles to keep your creation fireproof.

Never put your pumpkin on concrete; the concrete will suck out the moisture. Put a block of wood or piece of cardboard between the pumpkin and concrete if you are displaying them on a concrete patio, porch, or walkway.

## WORKING WITH FAUX PUMPKINS

I have grown my own pumpkins for years. Every Halloween season the family has an annual pumpkin carving night. We pick our pumpkin from the garden and get creative with designs. The guys get really competitive. I watch them have fun carving elaborate designs while I usually carve something simple.

I've always hated putting a lot of effort into creating something amazing that will rot and turn into mush.

Then came the faux carvable pumpkin. What a creation!

Suddenly I could get creative without worrying about my work of art rotting on my front porch. I can keep the faux pumpkins and re-use them to decorate every year.

Since this amazing discovery, I have made creations with a wide variety of faux pumpkins on the market.

There are many types of artificial pumpkins. If you plan to carve the pumpkin be sure they say that they are carvable. They are usually listed as craft pumpkins but should say on the tag or in the description that they are carvable.

The faux pumpkins range from super cheap $1 ones at Dollar Tree to mid-range ones at Michaels and Jo-Ann's to the most expensive and, in my opinion, best ones on the market for carving, Fun-Kins.

I've tried just about all of them.

I purchased mini-pumpkins on Amazon. They were created to be used as-is for decorating. They are foam inside with a shiny plastic outer shell. Not suitable for carving at all, but they work well enough for painting and adding fun things to the outside.

I was surprised that the foam pumpkins from Dollar Tree are hollow inside so you can technically carve them, though they are made up of foam balls, which are quite messy to cut. You won't get even smooth cuts, and the foam will stick to everything. But, you can create cute things with them very inexpensively. If you want to paint them, use acrylics because the pumpkins do not have a plastic shell, just foam, so many oil-based paints could cause the foam to melt.

The Ashland craft pumpkins from Michaels are great for decorating, but I found them a little hard to carve and etch. They come in a variety of colors and sizes, so if you can find black or white or another fun color you won't have to paint them.

OrientalTrading.com also carries a decent selection of faux pumpkins. The ones I bought were small five-inch pumpkins, perfect for creating mixed media crafts and small carvings.

By far the absolute best artificial carvable pumpkins I have tried are available on Funkins.com.

Fun-Kins look and feel like real pumpkins. They even carve like real pumpkins, without the squishy pumpkin guts inside. Fun-Kins are available in multiple sizes, shapes, and styles. They have several white varieties and one black style.

Fun-Kins can be carved with regular pumpkin carving tools, serrated blades, and even power tools, if you want to get crafty.

What I really love about Fun-Kins is that their skin is soft and pliable enough that you can easily transfer a stencil design to the pumpkin with just a ballpoint pen. Tape the pattern or stencil on to the pumpkin, then trace over it with a pen. It will leave the imprint in the pumpkin skin. No other faux pumpkin does this. I've tried. The outer shells are too hard.

No matter what type of faux pumpkin you cut into, I suggest wearing protective glasses, goggles, or a face shield so foam particles and dust do not get into your eyes and you are not breathing anything in. This is absolutely necessary if you use power tools, like a Dremel, where dust will be flying everywhere. Also be sure to cover your workspace for easy cleanup.

## WHY CHOOSE A PARTY THEME?

Every time I start planning an event, whether it is a birthday party, wedding, or Halloween party, the first thing I do is pick a theme.

Why? Because choosing a theme for your party creates a focus, a central idea that makes the rest of your party planning come together easily.

Everything will revolve around the theme so you know exactly what you are looking for. A theme makes it easier to zero in and plan efficiently, and you get to flex your creativity.

A theme will bring together all the elements—decorating, invitations, food, games, entertainment, costumes, cocktails—and it makes shopping online easier because you can use keywords and hashtags to find the perfect decor and accessories.

Once you choose a theme, you'll be surprised at how streamlined the planning process becomes. Things have a tendency to fall into place.

Choosing a theme also makes decorating easy.

But before you go out shopping, shop in your own home, 90 percent of the things I used for decorating the party themes featured in this book were found in my house. Old things in my basement, random things on shelves, items tucked away in boxes of Halloween decor. For instance, my husband has tons of fishing and boat stuff I used in the background of the Nightmare under the Sea decorations. All the bottles and jars for Dr. Frankenstein's Laboratory were found around my house; they were displayed on shelves or hiding in the basement. For Gothic Elegance, I used my friend's stash of things she had tucked away after years of hosting a vampire ball along with some of my own vampire-themed decor. Search your home; you'll probably be surprised at what you find that fits your party theme.

Need another reason to pick a theme? It's fun! Pick a theme you love that will resonate with your guests. Now get creative. Your friends will *ooh* and *aah* over your clever decor and costume while you enjoy the amazing party you put together.

*Pumpkins and Party Themes* showcases ten unique Halloween party themes with tips, tricks, and ideas for color palettes, decorations, activities, and costumes along with five coordinating DIY pumpkin designs per party theme that will really bring your Halloween event to life.

## ROASTED PUMPKIN SEEDS

*This roasted pumpkin seed recipe has an extra step of boiling the pumpkin seeds before roasting, which easily removes the membrane and plumps the seeds for fantastic results.*

### Ingredients:
- Pumpkin seeds
- 1–2 teaspoons olive oil
- Finely ground pink Himalayan salt; pepper
- Optional: other seasonings per your tastes

### Instructions:
1. Gather the seeds you saved after carving your pumpkins.
2. Rinse the seeds to remove the pumpkin guts and strings.
3. Preheat the oven to 400°F.
4. Boil water—about 2 cups of water to ½ cup of seeds. Add ½ teaspoon of salt per cup of water. Boiling removes excess gunk from the seeds, plumps them so they roast more evenly, and helps make them more digestible by stripping them of certain enzymes.
5. After boiling, place the seeds in a colander and rinse. Any remaining pumpkin particles and strings should be separated.
6. Place the seeds in a mixing bowl. Add 1–2 teaspoons of olive oil and salt and pepper to taste. Stir the seeds until they are evenly coated.

    Additional seasonings and spices may be added per your taste.
7. Spread seeds in a single layer on a cookie sheet or in a shallow roasting pan in the upper portion of the oven.
8. Bake until seeds begin to brown and are the hardness of your liking; 10–20 minutes depending on your oven and preference. Watch for a change in color. As they roast, pumpkin seeds change from gray to white to a golden brown. Once they reach a golden-brown color, you know they are done.
9. Leave the seeds to cool on a rack until you can safely handle them.

*After the initial roast, I like to toss some of the pumpkin seeds in a sweet and spicy mix of melted butter, Louisiana hot sauce, chili powder, and brown sugar. I roast them first, then put them in a bowl and add this mixture. If I put all this on to roast, they always burn. So, I roast, then add flavor, then I roast them again for just a minute or two to get the flavor to adhere to the seeds.*

# CHAPTER 2

# WELCOME TO DR. FRANKENSTEIN'S LABORATORY

Do you love classic Frankenstein horror movies? Then this party theme is for you. It combines novel elements and classic Frankenstein monster movie visuals into one fun party theme. Frankie and the Bride of Frankenstein will create a matched set of old-fashioned silhouette style portraits facing each other when they are complete.

## PUMPKINS

- Frankie

- Bride of Frankenstein

- Dr. Frankenstein (Mad Scientist)

- Smoking Test Tubes

- Bubbling Beakers

## DRY ICE SAFETY TIPS

- Never handle dry ice with bare hands. Always wear gloves.
- Never store dry ice in a sealed container, it can explode. Dry ice should be wrapped in a paper bag.
- Never leave children or animals unattended around dry ice.
- Be aware of symptoms of carbon dioxide poisoning. Make sure there is good air circulation. Higher levels of carbon dioxide are most likely to become dangerous at ground level first because cold sinks. Please keep an eye on pets and small children who are low to the ground.
- Avoid placing dry ice into empty glass containers or directly onto countertops. The temperature shock could cause cracks.
- Do not store dry ice in your freezer or refrigerator. It can throw off your thermostat and create buildup inside your appliance. Store dry ice in a ventilated cooler or insulated cardboard box.

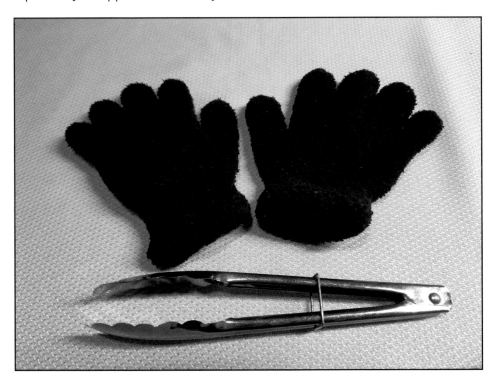

# Party Decor

## BRING YOUR PARTY TO LIFE WITH THIS ELECTRIFYING THEME

Envision an old-fashioned mad scientist lab full of flasks, beakers, test tubes, jars full of eyeballs and other creepy things, old science books, skeletons, body parts, old-fashioned electronics, and an ancient looking switch (for the bolt of electricity that brings the monster to life).

A plasma ball lamp would be a great touch with the flowing bolts of electricity lighting up the lab.

Use a fog machine or dry ice to create a foggy atmosphere.

And don't forget to have a copy of Mary Shelley's classic novel on hand.

# Color Palette

**GREEN   GRAY   BLACK   CREAM**

## DR. FRANKENSTEIN'S LABORATORY

# Activities

### YOUR GUESTS WILL HAVE A MONSTROUSLY GOOD TIME WITH THESE PARTY ACTIVITIES.

Set up a science lab themed drink mixing station featuring beakers and test tubes. There are some really amazing cocktail and mocktail recipes that would amp up the science part of this lab. Some make the colors of the drink change, some glow under black lights.

Have classic Frankenstein movies playing on a big screen TV in the background.

Put together a photo booth with fun Franken-themed props like skulls, severed limbs, lab coats, a Bride of Frankenstein wig, a mad scientist wig and mustache, and a Frankenstein's monster block head piece.

# Costume Ideas

**DR. FRANKENSTEIN  FRANKESTEIN'S MONSTER
BRIDE OF FRANKENSTEIN  IGOR**

# FRANKIE

## WHAT YOU'LL NEED:
- Average size pumpkin
- Frankie stencil template
- Ballpoint pen
- Blue painter's tape
- Serrated carving knife

## HOW TO MAKE IT:
1. Select an average size pumpkin. You can use a real pumpkin or a Fun-Kin. Make sure the outside is clean and dry.
2. Make a copy of the Frankie stencil (see stencil on pg. 172) with a ballpoint pen and attach it to your pumpkin with blue painter's tape.
3. Cut out the bolt and scar on Frankie with a serrated carving knife. You are creating a silhouette of Frankie, so you'll be cutting around him to cut out the background. Carefully cut out the background. You want the edges of Frankie's silhouette to be sharp so you can easily see it is Frankie. (Alternatively you can etch the background, which means you are carving into the pumpkin but not all the way through it.)
4. Once your pumpkin is carved, you can add a battery-operated candle or light. If you used a real pumpkin, you can clean it and add a preservative to prolong the life of the pumpkin.

# BRIDE OF FRANKENSTEIN

**WHAT YOU'LL NEED:**
- Average size pumpkin
- Bride stencil template
- Ballpoint pen
- Blue painter's tape
- Serrated carving knife

**HOW TO MAKE IT:**
1. Select an average size pumpkin. You can use a real pumpkin or a Fun-Kin. Make sure the outside is clean and dry.
2. Make a copy of the Bride of Frankenstein stencil (see stencil on pg. 173) with a ballpoint pen and attach it to your pumpkin with blue painter's tape.
3. Cut out the lightning bolts in the Bride's hair first with a serrated carving knife. You are creating a silhouette of the Bride, so you'll be cutting around her to cut out the background. Carefully cut out the background. You want the edges of the Bride's silhouette to be sharp so you can easily see it is the Bride of Frankenstein. (Alternatively you can etch the background, which means you are carving into the pumpkin but not all the way through it.)
4. Once your pumpkin is carved you can add a battery-operated candle or light. If you used a real pumpkin, you can clean it and add a preservative to prolong the life of the pumpkin.

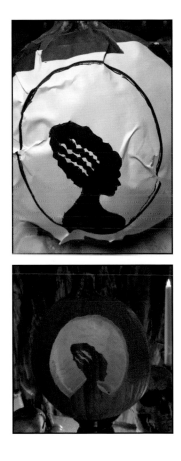

# DR. FRANKENSTEIN (MAD SCIENTIST)

## WHAT YOU'LL NEED:
- Average size pumpkin, more tall and thin than round
- Mad scientist wig and mustache set
- Steampunk goggles or safety goggles
- Sewing pins

## HOW TO MAKE IT:

1. Select an average size pumpkin. You can use a real pumpkin or a Fun-Kin. Make sure the outside is clean and dry.

2. Find a mad scientist wig and mustache set. These can easily be found at your local Halloween store, online costume stores, and on Amazon.

3. Put the steampunk goggles or basic safety goggles on the pumpkin and add the mustache and wig (you may need sewing pins to keep them in place).

# Smoking Test Tubes

**WHAT YOU'LL NEED:**
- Test tubes
- Mini pumpkins (real or foam, for this I used small craft foam pumpkins)
- Sharp knife or small saw
- Black spray paint
- Latex or nitrile gloves
- Green balloon lights
- Dry ice

**HOW TO MAKE IT:**
1. Start by taking your test tube and turning it upside down so the flat lip is over the top of your pumpkin. Then, trace the outline. This will be the area you cut out to place the test tube.
2. Use a knife or small craft saw and cut a hole deep enough in the pumpkin that the test tube will fit and not tip over. If the pumpkin is foam, scoop out the hole with your finger. If it is a real pumpkin, use a small spoon or butter knife to clear the hole.
3. Now it is time to spray paint your pumpkins black. Make sure you are in a well-ventilated area and that your workstation is covered so you don't get overspray everywhere. I paint outside then bring the items in to dry. Wear latex gloves to avoid getting paint on your hands. You'll probably need at least two coats to completely cover the pumpkin. Spray paint the hole. It may not stick well, but it will darken the inside so you don't have white or orange showing through your test tube.
4. Once your pumpkins are completely dry, you can test them out by dropping the small balloon light inside and then placing the test tube in the hole. You might need to dig into the hole a little more and create an alcove for the light.
5. Once light and test tube are in place, carefully pour hot water into the tube. Fill it about ¾ of the way full.

6. Use tweezers or tongs and drop a dry ice pellet into the tube. Now you have a bubbling, smoking test tube in your laboratory. The test tubes are small so the fog won't last long. Adding water and ice to the test tubes should be the last thing you do before the party begins. You'll need to refill them several times throughout the party to keep the effect flowing.

# Bubbling Beakers

## WHAT YOU'LL NEED:
- Small to medium pumpkins
- Black spray paint or acrylic paint
- Sponge paintbrush
- Latex or nitrile gloves
- Various size beakers
- Sharp knife or small saw
- Green balloon lights
- Dry ice

## HOW TO MAKE IT:
1. Choose pumpkins based on the size of your beakers. You want the pumpkins big enough to create a base that holds the beakers without having them so big the beaker is dwarfed by the pumpkin. Small, flat pumpkins are the best bet. If you choose real pumpkins, pie pumpkins are a good choice instead of traditional carving pumpkins.

2. Paint your pumpkins black. Real or large plastic-coated pumpkins can be spray painted, but foam pumpkins without a plastic coating should be painted with acrylic using a sponge paintbrush. I used foam pumpkins from Dollar Tree. They were the perfect size for the beakers, flatter rather than large and round. I painted them with black acrylic. If you use spray paint, make sure you are in a well-ventilated area and that your workstation is covered so you don't get overspray everywhere. I paint outside then bring the items in to dry. Wear gloves to

avoid getting paint on your hands. You'll probably need at least two coats to completely cover the pumpkin.

3. Once the paint is dry, take your beakers and trace their basic outlines on the top of the pumpkins. This will be the area you cut out to place the beaker.

4. Use a knife or small craft saw and cut a spot deep enough in each pumpkin so the beakers will fit snuggly and not tip over. Use a spoon or butter knife to clear the hole.

5. Once the pumpkins are cut, you may need to touch up paint. Spray paint the hole. It may not stick well, but it will darken the inside so you don't have white or orange showing through your beaker.

6. Once your pumpkins are completely dry, you can test them out by dropping the small balloon light inside and placing the beaker in the hole. You might need to dig into the hole a little more to create an alcove for the light.

7. When you are ready to use dry ice, make sure the light and beaker are firmly in place and carefully pour hot water into the beakers. Fill them about ¾ of the way full. Use tweezers or tongs and drop a dry ice pellet into the tube. Now you have bubbling, smoking beakers in your laboratory. The beakers are larger than the test tubes, but still won't last long. You'll need to refill them several times throughout the party to keep the effect flowing.

CHAPTER 3

# YOU'RE INVITED TO A BLOOD BASH

This vampire theme, with fun and horrific elements, is perfect for horror lovers and fans of vampire shows and movies like *True Blood*, *The Vampire Diaries*, *Van Helsing*, *Blade*, etc.

## PUMPKINS

- Nosferatu: Count Orlok

- I Vant to Suck Your Blood

- Sparkling Glitter Bats

- Coffin

- Blood Splatter

## YOU'RE INVITED TO A BLOOD BASH

# Party Decor

### HAVE A BLOODY GOOD TIME WITH THIS FANG FILLED PARTY THEME

Decorate with coffins, bats, blood splatter, and fangs.

Create a drink station with blood-themed cocktails, syringe shots, test tube shots, and blood bag drinks.

A Bloody Mary Bar would also be a great themed drink station.

# Color Palette

RED   BLACK   WHITE

## YOU'RE INVITED TO A BLOOD BASH

# Activities

### DIG UP VAMPIRE VILLAINS, MYTHS, AND LEGENDS TO CREATE FUN GAMES

Blood Splatter Art: set up a painting station with an easel, pad of art paper, and a covered floor (think of Dexter's plastic covered "work space"). Let guests splatter red paint on paper to create art.

Name That Fang: print out still shots of fangs from popular vampire movies and television shows. Post them on the wall or on a poster board with numbers. Have your guests fill out a little questionnaire with their guesses and put them in a coffin. The person with the most correct answers wins a prize.

# Costume Ideas

COUNT ORLOK   DRACULA   VAN HELSING   BLADE
WHISTLER   *TRUE BLOOD* CHARACTERS

# Nosferatu: Count Orlok

**WHAT YOU'LL NEED:**

- White Fun-Kin or real pumpkin
- Image of Count Orlok scene printed to fit your pumpkin
- Blue painter's tape
- Ballpoint pen
- Black acrylic paint
- Fine-tipped paintbrush

**HOW TO MAKE IT:**

1. Select an average size pumpkin. You can use a real pumpkin or a Fun-Kin. Make sure the outside is clean and dry.
2. Find a stock photo of a Count Orlok shadow scene or something similar and attach it to your pumpkin with blue painter's tape.
3. Take a ballpoint pen and trace the design on the pumpkin. Press firmly so the design imprints on your pumpkin. Fun-Kin Pumpkins have softer skin and the ballpoint easily leaves an impression, so your stencil or design shows through. If the skin of your craft pumpkin is too hard, you may need to use carbon paper or the dot-to-dot point method instead.
4. Remove the paper. Keep it intact because you might need to look at the original while you paint in case some lines are hard to see or didn't transfer.
5. Paint the design with black acrylic paint using a fine-tipped paintbrush. Alternatively you could use a black Sharpie to fill in the shadow design.

# I Vant to Suck Your Blood

**WHAT YOU'LL NEED:**
- Mini pumpkins (real or foam, for this I used small foam pumpkins)
- Sharp knife or small saw
- Black spray paint
- Latex or nitrile gloves
- Plastic vampire fangs
- Red acrylic paint, optional
- Red, green, or white balloon light, optional

**HOW TO MAKE IT:**
1. Start by taking your vampire fangs and positioning them on the pumpkin face where you would like them to be; now trace the outline.
2. Use a knife or small craft saw and cut a hole deep enough in the pumpkin that the fangs can be inserted and be slightly open. If the pumpkin is foam, scoop out the hole with your finger. If it is a real pumpkin, use a small spoon or butter knife to clear the hole to make enough space.
3. Now it is time to spray paint your pumpkins black. Make sure you are in a well-ventilated area and that your workstation is covered so you don't get overspray everywhere. I paint outside then bring the items in to dry. Wear gloves to avoid getting paint on your hands. You'll probably need at least two coats to completely cover the pumpkin. Spray paint the hole. It may not stick well, but it will darken the inside so you don't have white or orange showing through your fangs.
4. Attach the fangs to the hole. If you want to add a few blood droplets from the fangs and on the pumpkin, you can easily do this with red acrylic paint. Have small balloon lights? Red or white work best for this design. Place them in the hole with the fangs for an eerie glow.

# Sparkling Glitter Bats

**WHAT YOU'LL NEED:**
- Black spray paint
- Mini pumpkins
- Black glitter
- Mod Podge
- Foam brush
- Latex or nitrile gloves
- Thick black craft paper or black cardstock
- Scissors
- Push pins or sewing pins

**HOW TO MAKE IT:**
1. Spray paint your pumpkins black. Make sure you are in a well-ventilated area and that your workstation is covered so you don't get overspray everywhere. I paint outside then bring the items in to dry. Wear latex or nitrile gloves to avoid getting paint on your hands. You'll probably need at least two coats to completely cover each pumpkin.
2. While pumpkins are drying, trace and cut out your bat wings and ears (patterns for bat ears and wings can be found on pg. 183). Fold spots indicated by dotted lines.
3. Once your pumpkins are completely dry, you can start adding glitter. Grab your Mod Podge and a foam paintbrush. Coat the areas of your pumpkin you want to cover in glitter with Mod Podge. Shake glitter onto the Mod Podge areas. Shake off excess glitter onto a piece of paper. If you have bare spots, add more Mod Podge and glitter; shake off excess glitter. Repeat until your pumpkins are coated to your satisfaction. Place them somewhere to dry overnight. Do the same with the bat wings and ears.
4. Once everything is dry, attach ears and wings with sewing pins or small push pins.

# COFFIN

**WHAT YOU'LL NEED:**

- Wood craft coffin with hinges
- Craft pumpkin or Fun-Kin (I used a Boss Fun-Kin)
- Serrated carving knives or pumpkin saw (I used a small Kobalt hand saw)
- Spray paint in your chosen color
- Acrylic paint in your chosen color
- Glue
- Cameo or other decoration for the front of coffin
- Small Dracula or skeleton to fit inside coffin

**HOW TO MAKE IT:**

1. Purchase a small wood coffin with hinges. Craft stores like Michaels and Jo-Ann's always have a variety of them at Halloween. They can also be found on craft store websites like ConsumerCrafts.com and FactoryDirectCraft.com.
2. Select an average size craft pumpkin or Fun-Kin, large enough that the coffin will fit on the front. I used a large 17-inch Boss Fun-Kin.
3. Trace the coffin in the middle of the face of the pumpkin.
4. Cut out the coffin shape with a serrated knife, pumpkin saw, or small hand saw. Make sure the coffin fits snugly in the hole you cut out. If it fits snugly enough, you won't even have to glue it in.
5. If your pumpkin is not already the color you want (you can purchase faux pumpkins in white or black), spray

paint it in a well-ventilated area. I painted a large Fun-Kin with black spray paint and then used metallic red and metallic silver Rub 'n Buff to give it depth.

6.   Decorate your coffin. Paint it inside and out with acrylic paint. Once it is dry, decorate it with your cameo or findings of your choice.

7.   Glue the coffin in the hole if it doesn't fit snugly. Position it so the lid will open freely. You can put candy, treats, a small skeleton, or even a tiny mirror inside the coffin. I used a Tiny Treasures Dracula.

# BLOOD SPLATTER

This one is pretty easy, and you can have a lot of fun with it. White pumpkins, both real and fake, have become pretty easy to find around Halloween. For this, I used a white Fun-Kin. They have several sizes and styles on their website. You can also find white craft pumpkins at stores like Michaels and Jo-Ann's.

## WHAT YOU'LL NEED:
- White Fun-Kin or pumpkin painted white
- Plastic to protect work area
- Red acrylic paint
- Toothbrush or rough bristled paintbrush

## HOW TO MAKE IT:

1. Set up your pumpkin on a plastic drop cloth, grab thick red acrylic paint, and start splattering the pumpkin so it looks like blood drops and blood splatter. I suggest experimenting with methods and styles on paper first, determine which you like best, then move on to the pumpkin. One method is coating a toothbrush with the paint then using your thumb to flick the paint onto the pumpkin. Or, you can take a small paintbrush, dip it in paint, then flick paint at the pumpkin or let it drip off the brush.
2. Allow the paint to dry for your finished blood splatter look.

# CHAPTER 4
# SIMPLY BEWITCHING

This theme is open to creative interpretation because there are so many variables: witchy black and white, classic orange and black, fortune-telling, occult, and movie or television witch themes.

## PUMPKINS

- Pumpkins in Witch Hats

- Owl

- Cat

- Witch Boots

- Smoking Cauldron

## SIMPLY BEWITCHING

# Party Decor

## LEAVE YOUR GUESTS SPELLBOUND BY THIS BEWITCHING PARTY THEME

Decorate with witch hats, witch brooms, vintage Halloween decorations, sparkling glitter, potion bottles, black cats, owls, Tarot cards, crystal balls, apothecary jars, twisted tree limbs, flowers, spellbooks, and crystals.

# Color Palette

**ORANGE     BLACK     WHITE**

# Activities

## YOUR GUESTS WILL HAVE A BEWITCHING GOOD TIME.

Encourage guest creativity by having contests for the best broom, best witch hat, wickedest cackle, and best witches duo (or group) costumes.

Use Instagram aesthetics for inspiration and have Tarot or Oracle card readings, fortune telling, hold a séance, or have a Ouija board session.

# Costume Ideas

SABRINA   PRUDENCE   AUNT ZELDA   AUNT HILDA   THE SANDERSON SISTERS   SAMANTHA   WILLOW   THEODORA   ELPHABA

# Pumpkins in Witch Hats

**WHAT YOU'LL NEED:**
- Pumpkins
- Witch hats

**HOW TO MAKE IT:**

1. This one is super easy. Grab a bunch of pumpkins in varying sizes and a bunch of witch hats to match the pumpkin sizes. Combine. Now you have super cute pumpkins wearing witch hats. Of course, you can get creative by making your own hats or decorating pumpkins. Mix and match some of the other DIYs in this book with witch hats. I added a small witch hat to a glitter pumpkin.

# OWL

**WHAT YOU'LL NEED:**
- Pumpkin to fit stencil
- Owl stencil
- Blue painter's tape
- Ballpoint pen
- Carbon paper, optional
- Ice pick or pointed pumpkin tool
- Serrated carving knife

**HOW TO MAKE IT:**

1. Select an average size pumpkin. You can use a real pumpkin or a Fun-Kin. Make sure the outside is clean and dry.

2. Make a copy of the owl stencil (see stencil on pg. 174) and attach it to your pumpkin with blue painter's tape. If you use a faux pumpkin, you can transfer the stencil to the pumpkin with a ballpoint pen and carbon paper (if needed). For real pumpkins, I like to use the pointed pumpkin tool that looks like an ice pick to poke dots in the pumpkin through the stencil. I do this all around the edge of the areas to be cut out. This creates a connect-the-dots pattern for easy cut guidelines. No need to try to transfer the stencil to the pumpkin or cut through the paper.

3. Once your stencil is transferred or your dots are all punched through, remove the paper and carve with a serrated carving knife.

4. Once your pumpkin is carved, you can add a battery-operated candle or light.

5. If you used a real pumpkin, you can clean it and add a preservative to prolong the life of the pumpkin.

# CAT

**WHAT YOU'LL NEED:**
- Pumpkin to fit stencil
- Copy of stencil
- Blue painter's tape
- Ballpoint pen
- Carbon paper, optional
- Ice pick or pointed pumpkin tool
- Serrated carving knives

**HOW TO MAKE IT:**

1. Select an average size pumpkin. You can use a real pumpkin or a Fun-Kin. Make sure the outside is clean and dry.

2. Make a copy of the cat stencil (see stencil on pg. 175) and attach it to your pumpkin with blue painter's tape. Trace the black area of the stencil to be cut out. If you use a faux pumpkin you can transfer the stencil to the pumpkin with a ballpoint pen and carbon paper (if needed). For real pumpkins, I like to use the pointed pumpkin tool that looks like an ice pick to poke dots in the pumpkin through the stencil. I do this all around the edge of the areas to be cut out. This creates a connect-the-dots pattern for easy cut guidelines. No need to try to transfer the stencil to the pumpkin or cut through the paper.

3. Once your stencil is transferred or your dots are all punched through, remove the paper and carve with a serrated carving knife.

4. Once your pumpkin is carved, you can add a battery-operated candle or light.

5. If you used a real pumpkin, you can clean it and add a preservative to prolong the life of the pumpkin.

# Witch Boots

## WHAT YOU'LL NEED:
* Mini pumpkins
* Image of witch legs to print
* Scissors
* Toothpicks
* Glue
* Mod Podge
* Chunky glitter
* Fine black glitter

## HOW TO MAKE IT:
1. Select a couple of mini pumpkins.
2. Find a stock photo of witch legs or witch boots. Think of the witch legs you see sticking out of people's yards. This is the look you are going for. Adjust the size to fit your pumpkins and print them out.
3. Cut out the legs with scissors and attach them to toothpicks with glue.
4. While the glue dries on your legs, brush Mod Podge on the top of your pumpkins and sprinkle on the chunky glitter. Shake off the excess.
5. Add Mod Podge just to the boots of your witch and sprinkle on fine black glitter. Shake off excess.
6. Once all the glue is dry, stick your witch legs into the pumpkin. Now you have a mini pumpkin with tiny witch legs sticking out. Alternatively, if you have large witch leg Halloween decor, you can stick them directly in the pumpkin for a life-size version of this design.

# SMOKING CAULDRON

**WHAT YOU'LL NEED:**
- Fat, round pumpkin
- Black spray paint (if your pumpkin is not already black)
- Wine corks
- Serrated knife or small saw
- Paintbrush
- Black acrylic paint
- Handles
- Hot glue gun and glue sticks
- A bowl that fits inside the pumpkin
- Dry ice pellets

**HOW TO MAKE IT:**
1. Select a fat, round pumpkin. Cut the top off so you end up with a fat, round, cauldron shaped pumpkin. If your pumpkin is not already black, spray paint it black.
2. Select two wine corks that are the same size. Cut them into three even-sized pieces that will be the feet of the cauldron. I used a small hand saw to cut the corks. Paint the three pieces of cork black with acrylic paint to match the cauldron.
3. Select handles that look like cauldron handles. I had these round ones on hand that I picked up at a yard sale over the summer. They were absolutely perfect; they look exactly like something on the side of a witch's cauldron. If you don't have anything on hand, hardware and craft stores like Menards, Home Depot, Hobby Lobby, and Lowe's sell knobs and handles.
4. Push the screw through the pumpkin from the inside out. I used a screwdriver to make a hole, then pushed the screw through and attached the handles. If they are loose or wiggle too much, you can add a dab of glue to keep them in place.
5. Once the paint is dry on the corks, position them so that your pumpkin sits on them evenly. You want a firm stance so the pumpkin does not rock or tilt.

6    Add hot glue to the top of the corks and place your pumpkin firmly on the corks.

7    Find a bowl that fits inside the pumpkin. Add water and dry ice pellets (follow dry ice safety precautions on pg. 12). Now you have a smoking cauldron.

## CHAPTER 5
# GEAR UP FOR A STEAMPUNK ADVENTURE

Steampunk blends history, science fiction, steam-powered machinery, and futuristic elements to create an alternative history and a fun aesthetic. It is often depicted as an alternative Victorian era that blends traditional Victorian styles and elements with technology that did not exist back then. Steampunk is a fun theme that is wide open to creativity and personal interpretation. There are several movies that exemplify steampunk mechanics and devices that you can look to for inspiration: *The League of Extraordinary Gentlemen* (2003), *The Time Machine* (2002), *Sherlock Holmes* (2009), *Sherlock Holmes: A Game of Shadows* (2011), *Van Helsing* (2004), *Wild Wild West* (1999), and *The Golden Compass* (2007).

## PUMPKINS

- Geared Pumpkins

- Clock Pumpkin

- Teacups Full of Mini Pumpkins

- Steampumpkin with Top Hat and Goggles

- Copper, Gold, and Silver Pumpkins

## STEAMPUNK

# Party Decor

## IMAGINE WHAT NEVER WAS AND WHAT COULD NOT POSSIBLY BE

Decorate with gears, gadgets, goggles, cogs, clocks, top hats, and tea cups.

Envision the Victorian era all done up in bronze, gold, copper, brown, and black with a whole lot of mechanics thrown in.

Put your pumpkins on revolving cake or photography stands to create movement.

# Color Palette

• COPPER BRONZE GOLD SILVER BROWN BLACK •

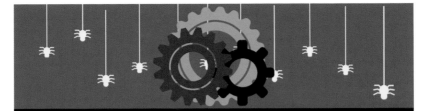

# Activities

## GEAR UP FOR A STEAMPUNK ADVENTURE

Play Traditional Victorian Parlor Games like Charades and Blind Man's Bluff

Steampunk Themed Board Games

Darts (use large gear shapes as targets)

Tea Time

Steampunk Mini Hat/ Fascinator Making Station

# Costume Ideas

VICTORIAN ENSEMBLES ACCESSORIZED WITH CORSETS  TOP HATS  GEARS  GADGETS  POCKET WATCHES  GOOGLES

# GEARED PUMPKINS

**WHAT YOU'LL NEED:**
- Small pumpkin
- Black spray paint
- Gears and other steampunk findings
- Hot glue and hot glue gun

**HOW TO MAKE IT:**
1. Select a small pumpkin and spray paint it black.
2. Find a variety of steampunk gears and accessories. These can be purchased at your local craft store or online.
3. When the spray paint is dry, hot glue a variety of the gears and finding to your pumpkin.

# CLOCK PUMPKIN

## WHAT YOU'LL NEED:
- Large faux pumpkin
- Black acrylic paint, optional
- Foam brush, optional
- Clock kit
- Small pumpkin knife
- Clock numbers
- Jewelry glue
- Gears
- Hot glue and glue gun

## HOW TO MAKE IT:
1. **Optional:** Paint the outer part of the pumpkin with black acrylic paint (use a foam brush) and leave the round "face" of the pumpkin orange. I did this to make the clock area stand out.
2. Purchase a clock kit at your local craft store or online. Some kits come with numbers; others are just the mechanical clock parts. I used one that included only the mechanical parts and purchased the numbers separately.
3. Cut a small hole in your pumpkin with a small pumpkin knife to insert the clock mechanism on the inside and the clock hands on the outside. Make sure this is in the center of the face of your pumpkin. You may have to scrape the inside of the pumpkin wall to make it thinner for the clock mechanism to fit properly.
4. Attach numbers onto craft gears with jewelry glue.
5. Attach the geared numbers with hot glue in the correct clock positions on the pumpkin. I started with 12 and 6, then 3 and 9. This creates the four main points so you can easily align the remaining numbers correctly.

# TEACUPS FULL OF MINI PUMPKINS

**WHAT YOU'LL NEED:**
- Tiny pumpkins that fit in the teacups
- Teacups and saucers

**HOW TO MAKE IT:**
1. Find pumpkins or fake pumpkins small enough to fit in teacups. I found glittered pumpkin picks at Dollar Tree. I took all the little pumpkins off the wood picks. This left me a nice jumble of teeny tiny pumpkins that fit into the teacups.
2. Place your pumpkins inside teacups. If you have a teapot you can create a cute tea display with the pumpkins.

# STEAMPUMPKIN WITH TOP HAT AND GOGGLES

**WHAT YOU'LL NEED:**
- Pumpkin
- Top hat to fit pumpkin
- Random gears, bolts, screws, and industrial findings
- Hot glue gun and glue sticks
- Steampunk goggles that fit on the hat or the pumpkin

**HOW TO MAKE IT:**
1. Select a pumpkin. I suggest a pumpkin that is human head-sized, that way normal size goggles and top hats will fit the pumpkin easily and you won't have to custom make those.
2. Find a top hat that fits on the pumpkin.
3. Get creative with leftover bits in the workshop. My husband has little bins of discarded bolts, screws, springs, and other objects that I used to create fun faces on my steampumpkin jack-o'-lanterns. Hot glue your pieces on to the pumpkin.
4. Add your top hat and goggles.

# COPPER, GOLD, AND SILVER PUMPKINS

## WHAT YOU'LL NEED:
- Black spray paint
- Mini pumpkins
- Latex or nitrile gloves
- Small cloths
- Gold leaf Rub 'n Buff
- Autumn gold Rub 'n Buff (Copper)
- Pewter Rub 'n Buff

## HOW TO MAKE IT:
1. Spray paint your pumpkins black. Make sure you are in a well-ventilated area and that your workstation is covered so you don't get overspray everywhere. I paint outside then bring the items in to dry. Wear gloves to avoid getting paint on your hands. You'll probably need at least two coats to completely cover each pumpkin.
2. Let them dry overnight.
3. Once the pumpkins are dry grab your cloths, gloves, and your gold, autumn gold, and pewter Rub 'n Buff. You should have a small cloth for each color. Squirt a dab of buff on the cloth then rub it onto the pumpkin. You want to leave some of the black showing through. This gives the pumpkins the aged steampunk look. Repeat this for each color pumpkin.
4. Let them dry overnight before touching or storing them.

# CHAPTER 6
# GOTHIC ELEGANCE

If you're an old-school Victorian goth or a fan of dark Victorian aesthetics, this party theme is for you.

## PUMPKINS

- Skull and Roses
- Red and Black Pumpkins
- Lace-Covered Pumpkins
- Sparkling Accents: Jewels
- Sparkling Accents: Glitter
- Dracula and Mina Silhouette

## GOTHIC ELEGANCE

# Party Decor

**WELCOME TO THE SANGUINARIAN SOIRÉE, A PARTY FOR VAMPS WITH DISCERNING TASTES.**

This one is for fans of old-school Goth aesthetics, Anne Rice's *Interview with the Vampire*, Bram Stoker's *Dracula*, and *Penny Dreadful*. This is old-school Victorian Goth at its best. Bustles and corsets, top hats and cloaks. I see this theme best suited for a fancy sit-down dinner or an elegant cocktail party.

Decorate your event with candles, lace, velvet— make it very elegant with hints of glitter and jewels to add to the decadence.

# Color Palette

RED  BLACK

**GOTHIC ELEGANCE**

# Activities

## TAKE YOUR GUESTS BACK IN TIME BY CREATING A NINETEENTH-CENTURY EVENT

The Victorian era was heavy on occultism.

Halloween parties were full of divination activities and sessions on communicating with the dead.

Hold a Nineteenth-Century Séance

Have a Ouija Board Session

Hire a Tarot Card Reader or Fortune Teller.

# Costume Ideas

*PENNY DREADFUL* CHARACTERS   DRACULA   MINA
ELEGANT VICTORIAN ATTIRE   LESTAT   LOUIS

# Skull and Roses

## WHAT YOU'LL NEED:

- Serrated knife
- 4-inch foam skull
- Black Fun-Kin
- Cutting board
- Paper plate
- Red acrylic paint
- Black acrylic paint
- Silver leaf Rub 'n Buff
- Liquid Stitch glue
- Lomey 2-inch diamanter corsage pins in red and clear (2 of each)
- Artificial red roses
- Scissors
- Hot glue gun and glue sticks

## HOW TO MAKE IT:

1. Use a serrated knife to cut your skull in half. You want it slightly rounded so it fits the curve of your pumpkin. Use a cutting board and go slowly so you don't split the skull.
2. Place the face of your skull on a paper plate or other surface and use red acrylic paint in the eyes. Cover the red of the skull with black acrylic. Be sure to use acrylic paint. Spray and other types of paint can make the foam disintegrate.
3. When the paint is dry, apply the silver leaf Rub 'n Buff with a clean soft cloth and coat the skull with silver. Leave some black and red showing through.
4. Next, glue the skull to your black Fun-Kin. I found that Liquid Stitch works really well with the foam skulls. Some glues will eat right through the foam. Liquid Stitch does not. Use red corsage pins in the eyes to hold it in place. I also used one clear corsage pin on the top and one on the bottom of

the skull to hold in place. Alternatively, you could use jeweled corsage pins all the way around the skull to give it a little more sparkle.

5    Grab your artificial roses and pop the heads off the stems. Cut the excess remaining stem off with scissors. You want the flower heads to sit flush on the pumpkin.

6    Experiment with the placement of the roses. Once you decide where you want them, add a dab of hot glue to the bottom of the rose and attach to the pumpkin.

# RED AND BLACK PUMPKINS

The methods for the following four styles all start the same, then branch out for customization.

## WHAT YOU'LL NEED:
- Mini pumpkins
- Black spray paint
- Red spray paint
- Latex or nitrile gloves

## HOW TO MAKE IT:
1. Spray paint your pumpkins in your choice of black or red (or both). Make sure you are in a well-ventilated area and that your workstation is covered so you don't get overspray everywhere. I paint outside then bring the items in to dry. Wear latex gloves to avoid getting paint on your hands. You'll probably need at least two coats to completely cover each pumpkin.
2. Let them dry overnight. Your red and black pumpkins exemplify understated Goth elegance. Place them on mantels, tabletops, buffet tables, and drink stations.

# LACE-COVERED PUMPKINS

**WHAT YOU'LL NEED:**
- Black spray paint (or use a black pumpkin)
- Red spray paint
- White spray paint (or use a white pumpkin)
- Pumpkins
- Latex or nitrile gloves
- Lace stockings or a piece of stretchy lace fabric large enough to wrap around your pumpkin (you can also use fishnet instead of lace)
- String
- Sparkling ribbon or cording
- Sewing pins

**HOW TO MAKE IT:**

1. Spray paint your pumpkins in your choice of black, white, or red (or use Fun-Kins that are already black or white). Make sure you are in a well-ventilated area and that your workstation is covered so you don't get overspray everywhere. I paint outside then bring the items in to dry. Wear gloves to avoid getting paint on your hands. You'll probably need at least two coats to completely cover each pumpkin.

2. Once your pumpkins are completely dry you can start customizing your designs. Take your pumpkin and either put it in the stocking or wrap it in your piece of lace. For a large pumpkin, I used the body area of the stocking. The leg portion just would not stretch enough. I put the pumpkin in the stockings and cut off the legs, then I pinned the extra fabric together on the bottom of the pumpkin. On the top, I gathered the waistband tight, stretched it, wrapped string around it, and tied it tight. Then I cut off the actual elastic waistband and pinned the fabric in place. Finally, I wrapped the black and white cord around the stem. To get the fabric stretched over the pumpkin and fitted correctly you are going to feel like you need extra hands, so you might grab a crafty

friend to help. I had pieces of ribbon and cord precut and ready to tie and sewing pins on hand to keep things in place. I also used my mouth to hold the ribbon and cord tight.

3. White, silver, or red lace can be used over black pumpkins, while black lace looks best over the red or white pumpkins (and is the easiest to find).

4. You'll want enough fabric left at the top of the pumpkin to gather and tie with ribbon. I suggest gathering it, tying it, and then cutting it.

5. For the mini and small pumpkins, you can easily slide them right into the toe of a pair of lace stockings. Stretch the lace then cut off that portion. Twist the lace then use ribbon or string to tie it tight. Stick a pin in where it won't be seen to hold in place. Now you can add your decorative ribbon or cording.

# Sparkling Accents: Jewels

**WHAT YOU'LL NEED:**
- Black spray paint
- Red spray paint
- Mini pumpkins
- Latex or nitrile gloves
- Sparkling corsage pins or push pins

**HOW TO MAKE IT:**
1. Spray paint your pumpkins in your choice of black and red (or both). Make sure you are in a well-ventilated area and that your workstation is covered so you don't get overspray everywhere. I paint outside then bring the items in to dry. Wear gloves to avoid getting paint on your hands. You'll probably need at least two coats to completely cover each pumpkin.
2. Once your pumpkins are completely dry you can start customizing your designs. Grab your pins and plan your design, then shove them into the pumpkin.

# SPARKLING ACCENTS: GLITTER

Glitter is easier to find than jeweled corsage pins or jeweled tacks, so this method may be an easier way to make your pumpkins sparkle.

## WHAT YOU'LL NEED:
- Black spray paint
- Red spray paint
- Mini pumpkins
- Latex or nitrile gloves
- Mod Podge gloss
- Foam paintbrush
- Fine red glitter
- Fine black glitter

## HOW TO MAKE IT:
1. Spray paint your pumpkins in your choice of black and red (or both). Make sure you are in a well-ventilated area and that your workstation is covered so you don't get overspray everywhere. I paint outside then bring the items in to dry. Wear latex gloves to avoid getting paint on your hands. You'll probably need at least two coats to completely cover each pumpkin.
2. Once your pumpkins are completely dry you can start customizing your designs. Grab your Mod Podge and a foam paintbrush. Coat the areas of your pumpkin you want to over in glitter with Mod Podge.
3. Shake glitter in your color choice onto the Mod Podge areas. Shake off excess glitter onto a piece of paper.
4. If you have bare spots, add more Mod Podge and glitter; shake off excess glitter. Repeat until your pumpkins are coated to your satisfaction. Place them somewhere to dry overnight.

# Dracula and Mina Silhouette

## WHAT YOU'LL NEED:
- Average size pumpkin
- Dracula and Mina stencil
- Blue painter's tape
- Ballpoint pen
- Carbon paper, optional
- Black acrylic paint
- Paintbrush
- Carving tools

## HOW TO MAKE IT:
1. Select an average size pumpkin. You can use a real pumpkin or a Fun-Kin. Make sure the outside is clean and dry.
2. Make a copy of the Dracula and Mina stencil (see stencil on pg. 176) and tape it to your pumpkin. Trace the design onto the pumpkin with a ballpoint pen. Press firmly to embed the design in the pumpkin skin so you can see where to cut.
3. If the ballpoint pen does not work (some pumpkins are too firm for the pen to show through, Fun-Kin pumpkins have soft skin so the design imprints well with just a pen), you'll need to either use carbon paper to transfer the image onto the pumpkin or use the dot method to get your design onto the pumpkin.
4. You are creating a silhouette, so you'll be etching around the figure to create a lighter colored background, but you are not cutting through the entire pumpkin, just cutting into it. Carefully etch out the background with your carving tool. I used a small tipped tool to cut around the silhouette to get

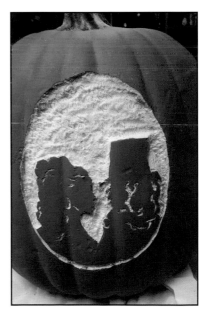

clean edges and a larger scooped one to cut out the background deeper. You want the edges of the silhouette to be sharp so you can easily see it is Mina and Dracula.

5. Once the pumpkin is carved, you can paint the silhouette area black to make it really stand out, You can also paint the entire pumpkin black. This makes it fit into the red and black decoration theme better than leaving it orange. If you use a faux pumpkin, you can brush black acrylic paint on the pumpkin. Be sure not to get any in the etched area.

6. You can also cut out the bottom and add a battery-operated candle or light.

7. If you used a real pumpkin, you can clean it and add a preservative to prolong the life of the pumpkin. I had a picture frame on hand that fit the pumpkin and cameo cutout perfectly, so I added it. If you have an old frame on hand that fits the design, this can be a fun detail to add.

## CHAPTER 7
# DOWN THE RABBIT HOLE

This one is for the *Alice in Wonderland* and *Alice through the Looking Glass* fans.

**PUMPKINS**

- Mad Hatter Top Hat

- Keys to Wonderland

- Queen of Hearts

- Cheshire Cat

- Playing Cards

## DOWN THE RABBIT HOLE

**Party Decor**

CURIOUSER AND CURIOUSER

Have fun and decorate with Mad Hatter top hats, tea pots and tea cups, chess set and chess pieces, playing cards, Cheshire Cat, Alice, the White Rabbit, red hearts, clocks, pocket watches, keys . . . create your own Wonderland.

**Color Palette**

RED   BLACK   WHITE

# Activities

## WE'RE ALL MAD HERE

Play Chess (could be a life-size game, have the guests be the chess pieces)

Have a Tea Party

Play Cards

Have *Alice in Wonderland* and *Alice through the Looking Glass* Movies Playing in Background

Create a Playlist of Alice Themed Songs

# Costume Ideas

ALICE    WHITE RABBIT    QUEEN OF HEARTS
CHESHIRE CAT    TWEEDLE DEE AND TWEEDLE DUM
THE CATERPILLAR    PLAYING CARDS    CHESS PIECES

# Mad Hatter Top Hat

**WHAT YOU'LL NEED:**
- Pumpkin to fit stencil
- Mad Hatter stencil
- Blue painter's tape
- Ballpoint pen
- Carbon paper, optional
- Etching tools

**HOW TO MAKE IT:**
1. Select an average size pumpkin. You can use a real pumpkin or a Fun-Kin. Make sure the outside is clean and dry.
2. Start by cutting out the bottom so you can add a battery-operated candle or light once the design is complete.
3. Make a copy of the Mad Hatter stencil (see stencil on pg. 177) and attach it to your pumpkin with blue painter's tape. If using a Fun-Kin, simply trace the design onto the pumpkin with a ballpoint pen. Press firmly to embed the design in the pumpkin skin so you can see where to cut. If the ballpoint pen does not work, you'll need to either use carbon paper to transfer the image onto the pumpkin or use the dot method to get your design onto the pumpkin.
4. For this stencil, you are etching out the black areas. Carefully etch out the areas with your carving tool. I used a small tipped tool to cut around the hat to get clean edges and a larger scooped one to cut out the larger areas.
5. If you used a real pumpkin, you can clean it and add a preservative to prolong the life of the pumpkin.

# Keys to Wonderland

**WHAT YOU'LL NEED:**
- 5-inch white pumpkin
- Scissors
- Red craft foam
- Mod Podge
- Foam brush
- Red glitter
- Five keys in various sizes
- Hot glue gun and glue sticks
- Four red plastic jewels

**HOW TO MAKE IT:**
1. Start with a 5-inch white pumpkin. I purchased one from OrientalTrading.com.
2. With scissors cut out a large heart on the red craft foam.
3. Brush Mod Podge with a foam brush onto the heart, then sprinkle with red glitter.
4. Once the glitter and glue have dried, hot glue the heart to the pumpkin.
5. Position one key in the middle of the heart and hot glue the key onto the heart.
6. Hot glue the remaining keys to your pumpkin, one on each side and one in the back.
7. Hot glue your four plastic jewels to the top of the pumpkin to line up with the placement of the keys

# Queen of Hearts

## WHAT YOU'LL NEED:

- 5-inch white pumpkin
- Red craft foam
- Scissors
- Tape
- Push pins, corsage pins, or sewing pins
- Acrylic paints in black, blue, and red
- Paper cups
- Gold spray paint
- Very fine-tipped paintbrush
- Mod Podge
- Foam brush
- Red and black glitter

## HOW TO MAKE IT:

1. Start with a 5-inch white pumpkin. I purchased one from OrientalTrading.com.
2. Trace the heart design on the red craft foam. With scissors first cut out the large heart, then cut out the center heart.
3. Position the heart on the pumpkin so it leaves an open area for the Queen's face. Pin the foam heart to the pumpkin at the heart point on top, the bottom heart point, and one on each side.
4. Paint the Queen's face on the pumpkin with acrylic paints in black, blue, and red using a very fine-tipped paintbrush. I found a photo of the Queen from the Tim Burton *Alice and Wonderland* movies and used her face as a reference—blue eyeshadow, thin eyebrows, and a tiny heart mouth.
5. While that paint dries, work on your crown. I used a paper cup from Dollar Tree where you can buy a pack of eight for $1. Your local discount store will likely have similar deals. Draw a line all the way around the cup about ⅓ to ½ down. This is your cut point. Cut triangles down to the line all the way around the cup. This creates the crown tips.

6.  Cut out small hearts (see Queen of Hearts pattern on pg. 184). Cut out enough for each crown tip to have one and one for the front of the crown. Glue these onto the crown.
7.  Spray paint your crown gold.
8.  Once the spray paint is dry, brush Mod Podge onto the hearts with a foam brush, sprinkle red and black glitter onto them, and then shake off the excess.
9.  Attach the crown to your Pumpkin Queen.

# CHESHIRE CAT

**WHAT YOU'LL NEED:**

- Craft pumpkin
- Paintbrushes
- White, black, pink, and teal acrylic paints
- Scissors
- Cheshire Cat stencil
- Scrap cardboard
- Cheshire Cat face printout
- Mod Podge
- Foam paintbrush
- Push pins, sewing pins

**HOW TO MAKE IT:**

1. Find a wide, flat pumpkin to best fit the shape of the Cheshire Cat. I used a foam craft pumpkin from Dollar Tree.
2. Start by painting the pumpkin gray. You can blend white and black to make gray, then add stripes of white and black throughout the pumpkin to give it a layered effect like the cat's striped fur. Add small blended stripes of teal around the face.
3. Using the cat stencil (see stencil on pg. 184), cut out the ears on a scrap piece of cardboard (cereal box cardboard is perfect). Paint the ears to match the pumpkin—gray, black, white, hints of teal. Add a bit of pink to the inside triangle of the ears.

4. While your paint dries, find and print out a Cheshire Cat face to match the size of the pumpkin. My printout was the eyes, nose, and mouth only. You can also paint these on, if you prefer. Cut out your features.
5. Make sure the paint is dry, then position the eyes, nose, and mouth on the pumpkin. Brush the Mod Podge with a foam paintbrush on the back of the cutouts; attach to the pumpkin. Brush the Mod Podge over and smooth the paper out.
6. Let everything dry.
7. Attach your ears to the top of the pumpkin with the push pins or sewing pins.

# PLAYING CARDS

**WHAT YOU'LL NEED:**
- Craft pumpkin
- White acrylic paints
- Foam paintbrush
- Serrated pumpkin blade
- Deck of playing cards
- Glue, optional

**HOW TO MAKE IT:**
1. Find a foam craft pumpkin. Foam pumpkins work best for this design because it is easy to slice thin cuts for the cards to slide into. I used one from Dollar Tree.
2. First, paint the pumpkin white with a foam paintbrush. You'll probably need a couple of coats. Once the paint is dry, start slicing staggered cuts into the pumpkin with a serrated pumpkin blade. Keep the slices thin.
3. Position the cards so they are sticking out all over the pumpkin. If you want them to be permanent, add glue to the bottom corner of each card before sliding it into the pumpkin.

# CHAPTER 8
# EDGAR ALLAN POE

Edgar Allan Poe is the master of the macabre. Fans of literary horror adore Poe. It is no surprise that he's a popular author to read at Halloween. Take that a step further and create a Poe party.

## PUMPKINS

- The Raven
- The Tell-Tale Heart
- Edgar Allan Poe
- The Black Cat
- Nevermore

# EDGAR ALLAN POE

# Party Decor

## CREATE A MACABRE MASTERPIECE

Set the spooky stage with a touch of elegance—use ravens, anatomical hearts, black cats, books, and book pages with Poe images and quotes.

Accessorize with old typewriters, parchment paper, vintage books, and old bottles.

Place skulls and ravens inside glass cloches.

# Color Palette

**BLACK   WHITE   RED**

# EDGAR ALLAN POE

# Activities

## A TELL-TALE PARTY THEME

Name that Poe Quote

Poe Trivia

Read Passages from Poe's Stories

Have Movies Based on Poe's Tales Playing in the Background.

# Costume Ideas

EDGAR   THE RAVEN   BLACK CAT   ANNABEL LEE   LIGEIA
RODERICK USHER   MADELINE USHER   AUGUSTE DUPIN
PRINCE PROSPERO   THE RED DEATH   A COURT JESTER   MONTRESOR

🎃 PUMPKINS AND PARTY THEMES

# THE RAVEN

**WHAT YOU'LL NEED:**
- Small white pumpkin
- Raven Halloween decoration
- Tube of glue with fine tip
- Black glitter
- Wire

**HOW TO MAKE IT:**

1. Select a small white pumpkin or paint one white, and find a Raven Halloween decoration.
2. Draw a swirly design on the pumpkin with glue. I used a tube of Liquid Stitch because it had a fine point for easy writing.
3. Shake black glitter onto the design. Shake off excess. Let the glitter dry thoroughly before attaching the raven to the top. You may need to wrap the wire around the raven's legs and pumpkin stem to hold it in place. Add a couple of dots of glue underneath the raven to further secure it to the pumpkin.

# THE TELL-TALE HEART

## WHAT YOU'LL NEED:
- Small- to medium-sized black Fun-Kin or craft pumpkin
- Anatomical heart mold
- Air dry Sculpey clay
- Red and black acrylic paint
- Paintbrush
- Hot glue gun and glue sticks

## HOW TO MAKE IT:
1. Select a black Fun-Kin or craft pumpkin to fit the size of your anatomical heart. My heart mold was small, so I had to find a smallish pumpkin.

2. Work the clay in your hands until it is soft and warm. Push into the mold. Press the clay firmly into the mold. Let it sit for a few minutes before gently popping it out of the mold.
3. Lay the heart somewhere to dry. It will be thick, so it may take a few days. Flip it over after twelve hours so it can dry on all sides. (Want it to dry faster? Purchase the Sculpey bakeable clay and it'll be ready to paint in two hours or less.)
4. Once the heart is dry, paint it red, add black around the edges, then smear some black through the red. Mix colors until the heart looks dark and gothic.

5. After the paint dries on the heart, use a hot glue gun to attach your heart to the center of your pumpkin.

# EDGAR ALLAN POE

**WHAT YOU'LL NEED:**
- White Fun-Kin or real pumpkin
- Image of Poe printed to fit your pumpkin
- Blue painter's tape
- Ballpoint pen
- Fine-tipped paintbrush
- Black acrylic paint

**HOW TO MAKE IT:**

1. Select an average size pumpkin. You can use a real pumpkin or a Fun-Kin. Make sure the outside is clean and dry.
2. Search online for a black and white digital rendering of Poe that will translate well into a black and white painting. I found this great black and white image of Poe on Pixabay.com.
3. Print out Poe, cut to fit, and attach to your pumpkin with painter's tape. This can be a bit tricky; you will get a few creases in the paper because the pumpkin is round.
4. Take a ballpoint pen and trace the design on the pumpkin. Press firmly so the design imprints on your pumpkin. If the skin of your fake pumpkin is too hard, you may need to use carbon paper or the dot-to-dot point method instead.
5. Remove the paper. Keep it intact because you might need to look at the original while you paint in case some lines are hard to see or didn't transfer.
6. Paint the design with black acrylic paint using a fine-tipped paintbrush. Alternatively, you could use a black Sharpie to fill in the shadow design.

# THE BLACK CAT

## WHAT YOU'LL NEED:
- Mini pumpkins
- Black spray paint
- Latex or nitrile gloves
- Scissors
- Black glitter
- Mod Podge
- Foam brush
- Thick black craft paper or black cardstock
- Push pins or sewing pins

## HOW TO MAKE IT:
1. Spray paint your pumpkins black. Make sure you are in a well-ventilated area and that your workstation is covered so you don't get overspray everywhere. I paint outside then bring the items in to dry. Wear latex or nitrile gloves to avoid getting paint on your hands. You'll probably need at least two coats to completely cover each pumpkin.
2. While pumpkins are drying, trace and with scissors cut out your cat ears (the pattern for black cat ears can be found on pg. 183). Fold spots indicated by dotted lines.
3. Once your pumpkins are completely dry, you can start adding glitter. Grab your Mod Podge and a foam brush. Coat the areas of your pumpkin you want to cover in glitter with Mod Podge.
4. Shake black glitter onto the Mod Podge areas. Shake off excess glitter onto a piece of paper.
5. If you have bare spots, add more Mod Podge and glitter, shake off excess glitter. Repeat until your pumpkins are coated to your satisfaction. Place them somewhere to dry overnight. Do the same with the cat ears.
6. Once everything is dry, attach ears with small push pins or sewing pins and Mod Podge.

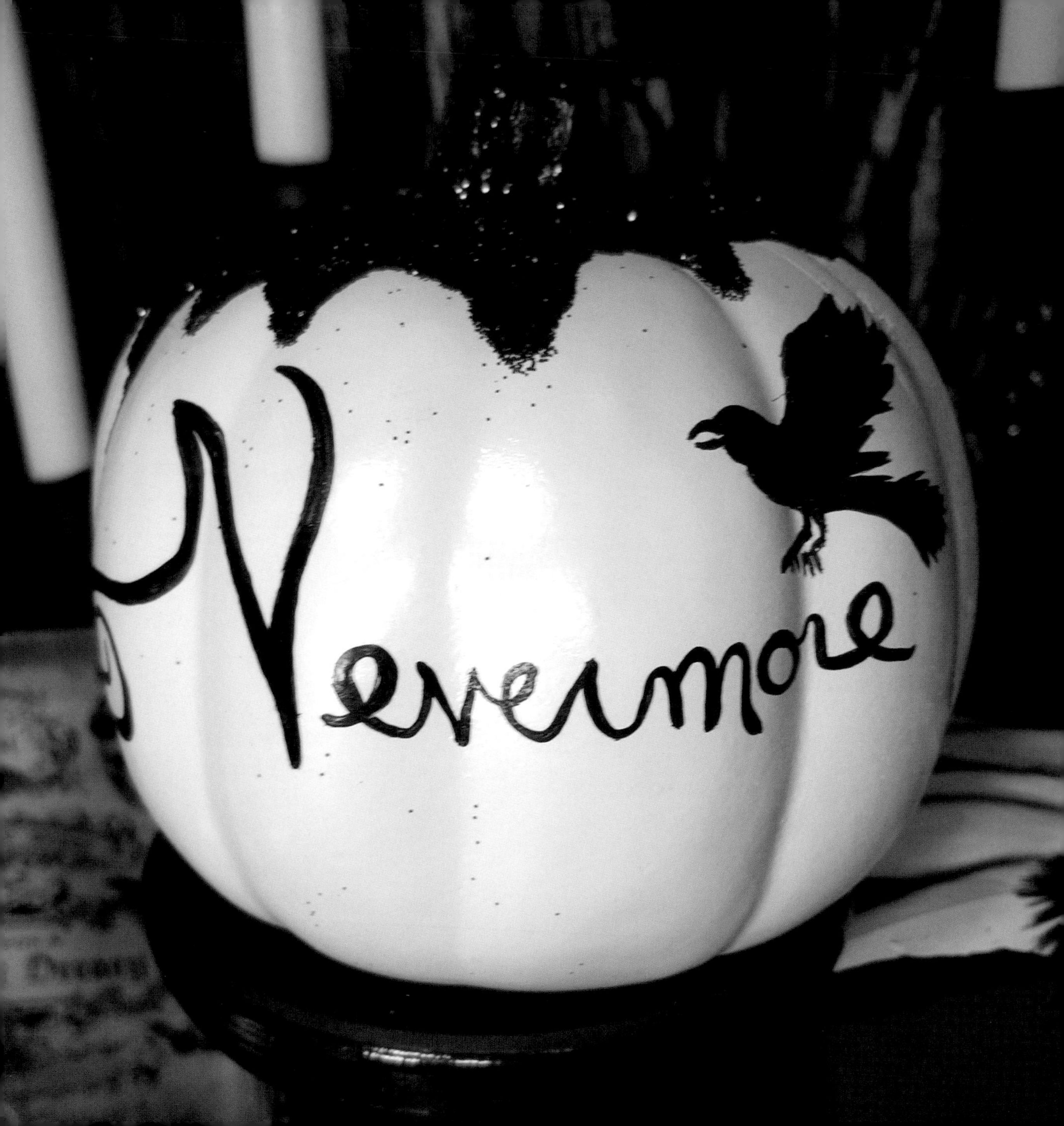
Nevermore

# Nevermore

**WHAT YOU'LL NEED:**
- Small pumpkin
- Ballpoint pen
- Fine-tipped paintbrush
- Black acrylic paint
- Fat-tipped paintbrush
- Mod Podge
- Black glitter

**HOW TO MAKE IT:**
1. Select a small- to medium-size white pumpkin. Make sure the outside is clean and dry.
2. You can either freestyle the lettering with a ballpoint pen or look up a font you like and print it out and transfer it to the pumpkin. I freestyled "Nevermore" with a pen onto the pumpkin, then drew a small raven silhouette.
3. After adding the letters and raven to your pumpkin, go over the letters and outline of the raven with a fine-tipped paintbrush and black acrylic paint. Fill the raven in with a fat-tipped paintbrush and black paint. Let everything dry, then add another coat of paint if needed.
4. Grab your Mod Podge and paint a design around the top of the pumpkin. Sprinkle black glitter into the Mod Podge. Make sure you paint the Mod Podge on thick so the glitter will adhere well.
5. Shake off excess glitter. Add more Mod Podge and glitter until the design is filled to your liking. Let dry.

# CHAPTER 9
# LET'S GET LITERARY

This one is for book lovers who love classic tales of terror. You can incorporate any books and authors you wish, but for this theme, the focus is on several classics: *Frankenstein* by Mary Shelley, *The Legend of Sleepy Hollow* by Washington Irving, *Dracula* by Bram Stoker, *The Call of Cthulhu* by H.P. Lovecraft, *The Strange Case of Dr. Jekyll and Mr. Hyde* by Robert Louis Stevenson, and the Sherlock Holmes books by Sir Arthur Conan Doyle.

## PUMPKINS

- Books

- The Legend of Sleepy Hollow:
  The Headless Horseman

- Sherlock Holmes

- Cthulhu

- Dr. Jekyll and Mr. Hyde

# LET'S GET LITERARY

## Party Decor

### A LITERARY LOVER'S PARADISE

Use books as centerpieces

Classic books—be sure to have copies of any story you
feature in your activities and decor.

Create book banners with quotes from the books

Add footprints on the floor (Follow the Clues mystery
theme)

Character silhouettes

Sherlock Holmes cap and pipe

## Color Palette

BLACK   BROWN   BURGUNDY   DARK GREEN
NAVY BLUE   GOLD   CREAM

# LET'S GET LITERARY

## Activities

### GAMES BOOK LOVERS WILL ADORE

Play "Name that Literary Quote"

Have Guests Participate in a Murder Mystery

Play Literary Themed Board and Card Games:
Papercuts—A Party Game for the Rude and
Well Read, The Storymatic Classic, 221 Baker
Street—The Master Detective Game, Bookopoly
Board Game, Lit Chat—Conversation Starters
about Books and Life

## Costume Ideas

ICHABOD CRANE   THE HEADLESS HORSEMAN   KATRINA VAN TASSEL
SHERLOCK HOLMES   DR. WATSON   DR. JEKYLL/MR. HYDE   CTHULHU
DR. FRANKENSTEIN   FRANKENSTEIN'S MONSTER   DRACULA   MINA   LIBRARIAN

# Books

**WHAT YOU'LL NEED:**
- Craft pumpkin or Fun-Kin (I used a Boss Fun-Kin)
- Three books: two of the same size, one larger
- Serrated carving knife, small handsaw, or pumpkin saw (I used a small pumpkin saw)

**HOW TO MAKE IT:**
1. Select an average size craft pumpkin or Fun-Kin, large enough that three books will fit inside. I used a large, 17-inch Boss Fun-Kin.
2. Hold the books together. Place the largest in the middle with the smaller ones on each side. Trace the book shapes in the middle of the face of the pumpkin.
3. Cut out the book shape with a serrated knife, small handsaw, or pumpkin saw.
4. Make sure the books fit snugly in the hole you cut out.
5. If your pumpkin is not already the color you want (you can purchase faux pumpkins in white or black), spray paint it in a well-ventilated area. I painted a large Fun-Kin with black spray paint, then used metallic red and metallic silver Rub 'n Buff to give it depth.
6. You may need to place a rock or something heavy inside the pumpkin before putting your books in. This counterbalances the pumpkin so it doesn't fall over from the weight of the books on one side.

# THE LEGEND OF SLEEPY HOLLOW: THE HEADLESS HORSEMAN

## WHAT YOU'LL NEED:

- Average size pumpkin
- Headless horseman stencil
- Ballpoint pen
- Blue painter's tape
- Carbon paper, optional
- Paintbrush
- Black acrylic paint
- Carving tools

## HOW TO MAKE IT:

1. Select an average size pumpkin, you can use a real pumpkin or a Fun-Kin. Make sure the outside is clean and dry.
2. Make a copy of the headless horseman stencil (see stencil on pg. 178) and attach it to your pumpkin with blue painter's tape. Trace the design onto the pumpkin with a ballpoint pen. Press firmly to embed the design in the pumpkin skin so you can see where to cut. If the ballpoint pen does not work (some pumpkins are too firm for the pen to show through, Fun-Kin pumpkins have soft skin so the design imprints well with just a pen), you'll need to use carbon paper to transfer the image onto the pumpkin.
3. Once the design is on your pumpkin, with a paintbrush paint the horse and rider black.
4. Alternatively, this stencil is designed that you can carve it if you have a large enough pumpkin and a small enough blade. Carve out the gray areas. Start with the smallest inside areas first, then cut from the top down. Cut in small sections inside to outside one piece at a time. Do not cut the entire circle then work in. This will make the pumpkin weak, and it will fall apart.

# SHERLOCK HOLMES

## WHAT YOU'LL NEED:
- Average size pumpkin
- Sherlock stencil
- Ballpoint pen
- Blue painter's tape
- Black acrylic paint
- Paintbrush
- Carving tools

## HOW TO MAKE IT:
1. Select an average size pumpkin, you can use a real pumpkin or a Fun-Kin. Make sure the outside is clean and dry.
2. Make a copy of the Sherlock stencil (see stencil on pg. 179) and attach it to your pumpkin with blue painter's tape. Trace the design onto the pumpkin with a ballpoint pen. Press firmly to embed the design in the pumpkin skin so you can see where to cut.
3. You are creating a silhouette of Sherlock, so you'll be etching around him to create a lighter colored background. You are not cutting out the entire pumpkin, just cutting into it. Carefully etch out the background with your carving tools. I used a small tipped tool to cut around Sherlock's silhouette to get clean edges and a larger scooped one to cut out the background deeper. You want the edges of Sherlock's silhouette to be sharp so you can easily see it is Sherlock Holmes.

4. Once the pumpkin is carved you can paint the silhouette area black with a paintbrush to make it really stand out. You can also cut out the bottom and add a battery-operated candle or light. If you used a real pumpkin, you can clean it and add a preservative to prolong the life of the pumpkin.

# CTHULHU

**WHAT YOU'LL NEED:**
- Average size pumpkin
- Cthulhu stencil
- Ballpoint pen
- Blue painter's tape
- Carbon paper, optional
- Paintbrush
- Black acrylic paint

**HOW TO MAKE IT:**

1. Select an average size pumpkin. You can use a real pumpkin or a Fun-Kin. Make sure the outside is clean and dry.

2. Make a copy of the Cthulhu stencil (see stencil on pg. 180) and attach it to your pumpkin. Trace the design onto the pumpkin with a ballpoint pen. Press firmly to embed the design in the pumpkin skin so you can see where to cut. If the ballpoint pen does not work (some pumpkins are too firm for the pen to show through; Fun-Kin pumpkins have soft skin so the design imprints well with just a pen), you'll need to use carbon paper to transfer the image onto the pumpkin.

3. Once the design is on your pumpkin, with a paintbrush paint the silhouette area black.

# DR. JEKYLL AND MR. HYDE

**WHAT YOU'LL NEED:**
- Average size pumpkin
- Jekyll and Hyde stencil
- Ballpoint pen
- Blue painter's tape
- Carbon paper, optional
- Black acrylic paint
- Paintbrush

**HOW TO MAKE IT:**
1. Select an average size pumpkin. You can use a real pumpkin or a Fun-Kin. Make sure the outside is clean and dry.
2. Make a copy of the Jekyll and Hyde stencil (see stencil on pg. 181) and attach it to your pumpkin with blue painter's tape. Trace the design onto the pumpkin with a ballpoint pen. Press firmly to embed the design in the pumpkin skin so you can see where to cut. If the ballpoint pen does not work (some pumpkins are too firm for the pen to show through; Fun-Kin pumpkins have soft skin so the design imprints well with just a pen), you'll need to use carbon paper to transfer the image onto the pumpkin.
4. Once the design is on your pumpkin, paint the silhouette area black.

# CHAPTER 10

# ZOMBIES AND GHOULS

A zombies and ghouls party theme is for fans of zombie movies and *The Walking Dead*. This party theme can get a little bloody, gruesome, and horrific depending on your style.

## PUMPKINS

- Zombies
- Hand Reaching Out
- Graveyard
- Brains
- Bloody Handprints

## ZOMBIES AND GHOULS

# Party Decor

### YOUR GUESTS WILL HAVE A GHOULISH GOOD TIME

Are zombies rising from their graves?

Use gravestones, broken coffins, creepy cloth, old ripped clothing, body parts, eyeballs, blood splatter, and brains to set the scene.

Is the zombie outbreak a virus gone wrong?

Use caution tape, containment signs, virus outbreak signs, oozing green goo, hazmat suits, medical props, test tubes, and green lights to create an outbreak.

# Color Palette

### GREEN   BLACK   GRAY

## ZOMBIES AND GHOULS

# Activities

## DO THE ZOMBIE SHAMBLE

Play name that zombie movie

Have classic zombie movies playing on a big screen or *Walking Dead* episodes playing continuously

Brain toss—create a brain toss game by setting up several large cups or bowls and toss brain shaped balls into them. Assign each bowl a point value. The person with the most points wins a prize.

Zombie Paintball or Zombie Nerf—set up zombie targets to shoot with paintball guns

# Color Palette

ZOMBIES   GHOULS   ZOMBIE HUNTERS   FAMOUS MOVIE ZOMBIES
RICK GRIMES   DARYL DIXON
CHARACTERS FROM ZOMBIE MOVIES, TV SHOWS, & BOOKS

# ZOMBIES

## WHAT YOU'LL NEED:
- White Fun-Kin or real pumpkin
- Images of zombie silhouettes printed to fit your pumpkin
- Blue painter's tape
- Ballpoint pen
- Carbon paper, optional
- Black and green acrylic paints
- Fine-tipped paintbrush

## HOW TO MAKE IT:
1. Select an average size pumpkin. You can use a real pumpkin or a Fun-Kin. Make sure the outside is clean and dry.
2. Print out the shambling zombies and attach them to your pumpkin with blue painter's tape.
3. Take a ballpoint pen and trace the design on the pumpkin. Press firmly so the design imprints on your pumpkin. If the skin of your pumpkin is too firm for the ballpoint to make an indent, you may need to use carbon paper or the dot-to-dot point method. Use a red or colorful ink so you can see where you have traced over the black design.
4. Remove the paper. Keep it intact because you might need to look at the original while you paint in case some lines are hard to see or didn't transfer.
5. Paint the design with a fine-tipped paintbrush with black acrylic paint. I added black and green globs of paint around the top stem of the pumpkin and let them run down. Alternatively, you could use black and green Sharpies to fill in the shadow design.

# HAND REACHING OUT

## WHAT YOU'LL NEED:
- Pumpkin of your choice
- Fake severed hand
- Tiny wood stakes or large nails
- Wire
- Glue
- Red acrylic paint
- Cardboard, foam, or wood tombstones

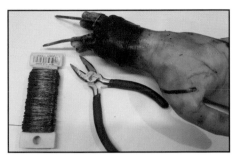

## HOW TO MAKE IT:
1. Select an average size pumpkin of your choice. You can use a real pumpkin or a Fun-Kin.
2. Find or make a fake severed hand and attach it to your pumpkin. How to do this really depends on the weight of the hand and the density of the pumpkin. You might have a hand with a stake already attached. The one I used for this design did not have a stake. For a small pumpkin like the one pictured, insert two tiny wood stakes or two large nails into the pumpkin and wire them to the hand. It is best to hammer the nails into the pumpkin to make the holes, then pull the nails out while you wire them to the hand. Once the wires are firmly attached, you can stick the nails back into the pumpkin and arrange everything how you want. Add a few dabs of glue for extra stability If your hand is not stiff enough to stay upright on its own, add a large craft stick behind the hand to hold it upright. Once your craft stick is in place, wrap wire around the wrist of the hand and the stick. This will hold the design firmly in place.
3. Squirt red acrylic paint over all the wires to hide them, then squirt red paint at the bottom of the hand and let it drip down the pumpkin.
4. Once the paint is dry, you can create a graveyard scene with tombstones. Arrange them with the pumpkin in the front.

# GRAVEYARD

**WHAT YOU'LL NEED:**
- Average size pumpkin
- Graveyard stencil
- Ballpoint pen
- Blue painter's tape
- Serrated carving knife
- Method to transfer stencil

**HOW TO MAKE IT:**
1. Select an average size pumpkin. You can use a real pumpkin or a Fun-Kin. Make sure the outside is clean and dry.
2. Make a copy of the graveyard stencil (see stencil on pg. 182) using a ballpoint pen and attach it to your pumpkin with blue painter's tape. Transfer stencil to your pumpkin.
3. Cut out the black area of the stencil with a serrated carving knife.
4. Once your pumpkin is carved you can add a battery-operated candle or light. If you use a real pumpkin, you can clean it and add a preservative to prolong the life of the pumpkin.

# Brains

**WHAT YOU'LL NEED:**
- Fake brain
- Pumpkin of your choice
- Small serrated knife or saw
- Glue
- Fake blood or red paint

**HOW TO MAKE IT:**
1. Find a toy brain. You want it to be a little squishy so you can push it into the pumpkin hole.
2. Select a pumpkin that is larger than the brain.
3. Cut off the top of the pumpkin with a small serrated knife or saw. You want the pumpkin large enough to fit the brain inside with a little bit of the top remaining to hold it in place.
4. Squish the brain in the hole. If it fits tight, then no glue is needed. If it wiggles and doesn't want to stay put, you'll need glue to help keep it in place.
5. Use red paint or fake blood to create blood oozing and dripping from the brain down the pumpkin.

# BLOODY HANDPRINTS

**WHAT YOU'LL NEED:**
- White Fun-Kin or pumpkin painted white
- Plastic to protect work area
- A couple shades of red acrylic paint

**HOW TO MAKE IT:**

1. Set up your pumpkin on a plastic drop cloth. Take your red paints and squeeze a few drops of each into your hand. You may want to add a few drops of black to the edges of your hands, but don't blend the colors or you'll end up with reddish-purple.
2. Brush your hand with a large sponge paintbrush to get the paint all over your palm and fingers.
3. Firmly press your hand on the pumpkin to leave a bloody handprint. If your pumpkin is large you can do this to both hands and leave multiple handprints.
4. Squirt red paint all around the top of the pumpkin and let it drip down.

# CHAPTER 11
# NIGHTMARE UNDER THE SEA

There are some truly creepy creatures in the ocean. Use them to create a "nightmare under the sea" party featuring the darker depictions of mermaids, sirens, tentacles, and sea monsters.

## PUMPKINS

- Mermaid

- Sea Shells

- Sea Horse

- Glitter Fish and Sea Creatures

- Kraken

# Party Décor

## DIVE INTO A NIGHTMARE

You can create incredible Nightmare under the Sea decor using any of these features: dark mermaids, scary octopuses, creepy sea horses, weird fish, shells, black lights, water features, pirate ships, pirates, star fish, tentacles, sea monsters, skeletons, broken boats, fishing poles, fishing nets, submarines, sunken ships, or ghost ships.

Create edible centerpieces or decorative candy bowls with Swedish fish and candies in multiple shades of blue and teal.

# Color Palette

TEAL/AQUA  PURPLE  BLUE  SILVER  GOLD  BLACK
SHIMMERING METALLICS

## NIGHTMARE UNDER THE SEA

# Activities

## YOUR GUESTS WILL HAVE A SWIMMINGLY GOOD TIME

Hidden Treasure—create a station where guests can decorate a treasure chest, then go on a treasure hunt to fill it. Have small items hidden in plain sight for guests to find like chocolate coins, candy pearls, seashell shaped mini notepads, mermaid pens . . . for an adults only party you could also hide mini bottles of booze.

Sea Shell Wind Chime DIY Station

Trivia Game Mermaid or Siren—give facts that pertain to one or the other (or both) and have guests guess which is which.

"Can you name that sea creature?"—showcase images of some of the weirdest and scariest things found in the ocean.

Set up a message in a bottle craft station.

# Costumes

**MERMAID   MERMAN   SEAHORSE   OCTOPUS   SEA MONSTER
PIRATE   SHIP CAPTAIN   SIREN   SHARK   DOLPHIN   FISH**

# MERMAID

## WHAT YOU'LL NEED:
- Pumpkin
- White acrylic paint
- Metallic blue acrylic paint (I used Americana Dazzling Metallics in "Ice Blue")
- Green acrylic paint (I used Americana "Irish Moss")
- Scale stencil
- Blue painter's tape
- Gold Rub 'n Buff
- Silver Rub 'n Buff
- Paintbrush or small cloth for the Rub 'n Buff
- Paint sponge brush
- Metallic aqua acrylic paint
- Fine-tipped paintbrush
- Glitter paint or glitter glue
- Two flat-sided seashells
- Hot glue gun and glue stick

## HOW TO MAKE IT:
1. Select an average size pumpkin. You can use a real pumpkin or a Fun-Kin. Make sure the outside is clean and dry.
2. Paint the pumpkin with blue and green acrylic paint. Mix and blend them. You just want a thin coat. Add a little white.
3. Once the acrylic paint is dry, find a stock photo of a scale and attach it to your pumpkin with blue painter's tape. Dab on small amounts of gold and silver Rub 'n Buff with a paintbrush or small cloth to fill in the stencil scales, alternating colors. Do this around the bottom of the pumpkin to create a scale pattern that represents the mermaid's tail.

5.  When the gold and silver are dry, you can hand-paint some scale outlines with a fine-tipped paintbrush with blue and aqua paint to make them stand out more. Then add glitter glue.
6.  On the top portion of the pumpkin figure out where you want to place the two shells. These will be the mermaid's bra. Hot glue them to the pumpkin.

# SEA SHELLS

**WHAT YOU'LL NEED:**
- Small to average size pumpkin
- Blue spray paint
- White spray paint
- Hot glue gun and glue sticks
- Sea shells
- Nitrile gloves

**HOW TO MAKE IT:**
1. Select a small to average size pumpkin.
2. Spray paint the pumpkin blue with a touch of white (like seafoam).
3. Once the paint is dry, hot glue seashells to the pumpkin. Wear latex gloves to avoid getting glue on your hands. You can create a pattern or just glue them on randomly.

# SEAHORSE

**WHAT YOU'LL NEED:**
- Pumpkin
- Seahorse stencil
- Painter's tape
- Texture paste
- Black spray paint
- Color shift spray paint or metallic acrylic paint
- Small putty knife
- Metallic acrylic paints in blue, teal, purple, and silver
- Fine-tipped paintbrushes

**HOW TO MAKE IT:**
1. Find a pumpkin that your stencil will fit on.
2. Find a stock photo of a seahorse and attach it to your pumpkin with blue painter's tape. I prefer this type of tape because it sticks when you want it to, but peels away easily without residue when you are done.
3. Make sure the stencil is firmly in place and carefully apply your texture paste in smooth, firm strokes. You want to fill the stencil without pulling it out of place. This is much trickier on a round, textured pumpkin than it is on a flat surface. It might take a few tries to perfect. That's all right. You can repeat the process all the way around the pumpkin with your seahorse stencil.
4. After the paste dries, spray paint the pumpkin black. Once that is dry, paint with a color shift spray paint. Alternatively, you can hand paint the pumpkin with metallic acrylics. I used Dupli-Color "Custom Wrap Effects Stellar Blue" because it was the

only paint I could find with the "under the sea" color theme I wanted. Rust-Oleum and other brands have color shift products, but they were not available in my local stores.

5. When the paint is dry, use the acrylic paints and with fine-tipped paintbrushes go over the raised designs. Get creative with the colors; make them stand out. A little goes a long way, so don't put too much paint on the brush. You want just the raised parts to stand out, not the entire design.

# Glitter Fish and Sea Creatures

## WHAT YOU'LL NEED:
- Pumpkin
- "Seaside" Rust-Oleum spray paint
- Sponge paintbrush
- Metallic acrylic paints in blue, teal, purple, and silver
- Printed silhouettes of fish, shark, dolphin, octopus, etc.
- Blue painter's tape
- Ballpoint pen
- Fine-tipped paintbrush
- Mod Podge
- Mermaid glitter (I used Darice "Chunky Glitter Mermaid Mix")

## HOW TO MAKE IT:
1. Select a large pumpkin.
2. Spray paint the pumpkin with "Seaside" color spray paint. Let it dry.
3. Sponge acrylic metallic blue, teal, purple, and silver onto the pumpkin. This gives it a shimmery effect. Let the paint dry.
4. Find silhouette images of a fish, shark, dolphin, starfish, octopus, etc. and print them out to fit your pumpkin.
5. Cut out each silhouette. Don't cut out the shape; just cut out squares or rectangle papers. You want your design to be centered on white space so you can tape it to your pumpkin.
6. Attach a silhouette to your pumpkin with blue painter's tape. Trace the shape onto your pumpkin with a ballpoint

pen. Press firmly so the shape comes through. Trace all your shapes onto the pumpkin.

7   Get a fine-tipped paintbrush and Mod Podge. Paint the Mod Podge into the shape, fill the entire shape with the glue, then sprinkle the glitter into the Mod Podge. Shake off the excess. If you work over a sheet of paper, you can curve up to funnel the glitter back into the container.

8   Repeat this for each shape. Only glue and glitter one at a time or your Mod Podge will dry out before you glitter them all. Return all excess glitter to your glitter container when finished.

# KRAKEN

**WHAT YOU'LL NEED:**
- Mini pumpkin
- Black spray paint
- Plastic to protect work area
- Latex or nitrile gloves
- Metallic blue, aquamarine, and silver acrylic paints
- Small paintbrush
- Hot glue gun and glue sticks
- Small Kraken (I found these buttons at Jo-Ann's, they are listed online as Steampunk 7 pk Octopus Buttons-Antique Gold)

**HOW TO MAKE IT:**

1. Spray paint your mini pumpkin black. Remember to paint outside or in a well-ventilated area. Cover your space with plastic or a painter's tarp. Wear gloves to protect your skin.
2. Once the pumpkin is dry, use the metallic blue and metallic aquamarine paints. With a small paintbrush, brush the paint on lightly so the black still shows through. You want the paint to be semi-translucent. The effect you are going for is similar to an oil slick. I alternating colors on each pumpkin section.
3. Once the acrylic paint is dry, hot glue your buttons on the pumpkin.
4. Lightly brush the silver paint over the Kraken so it is more silvery than antique gold. The silver will match the cool tone of the blue and aqua.

# ACKNOWLEDGMENTS

This book could not have been completed without the help and support of my family: Robert, Tim, Ari, Robby, and my mother, ClaraBelle. Their patience and love were a driving force of inspiration, and their cheerleading kept me going. *Thank you all for being there for me.*

A huge thank-you to my husband, Robert, who played an instrumental role in making sure this book was completed, especially when he played pack mule carrying all my boxes and boxes of supplies back and forth from our home to my temporary photo studio and drove all over town collecting supplies I needed. *I love you!*

Thank you to my daughter, Ari, who took my sketches and transformed them into digital designs for the stencils and patterns. Your digital design work is truly appreciated. *Love you!*

A major thank-you to my best friend Ilona, who had my back every step of the way during the book creation—from start to finish. She also provided gorgeous props and backdrops for several of the party themes. Thank you so much for listening to me vent when I was frustrated and for being my cheerleader when I needed a moral boost. *Love you always!*

Thank you to Fun-Kins for providing many of the artificial carvable pumpkins used to showcase the designs.

And thank you to Renee at Stockton House for renting me office space so I could create a photo studio to stage the party themes.

# APPENDIX:
# STENCILS AND
# ADDITIONAL PATTERNS

To use the following templates, scan each image. Open scanned image in a photo editing program. Adjust size to fit your pumpkin, then print.

- Frankie Stencil
- Bride Stencil
- Owl Stencil
- Cat Stencil
- Mini and Drac Stencil
- Mad Hatter Stencil
- Headless Horseman Stencil
- Sherlock Stencil
- Cthulhu Stencil
- Jekyll and Hyde Stencil
- Graveyard Stencil
- Bat and Black Cat Patterns
- Queen of Hearts and Cheshire Cat Patterns